In This Maybe
Best of All Possible Worlds

Poems by
William Page

Winner of 2016
futureCycle Poetry Book Prize

FUTURECYCLE PRESS
www.futurecycle.org

Library of Congress Control Number: 2016939539

Published by FutureCycle Press
Lexington, Kentucky, USA

ISBN 978-1-938853-99-9

For Elizabeth & Stephen

Contents

III. The Garden of His Shadow

Acknowledgments

I. Bullets

This Is Not

This is not about sad mothers.
It's not about a swirling Roman candle's
orange and blue balls of fire bursting
in crimson waves in a startled sky.
The small-boned boy does not float easily
in the blue water lapping against the white
pool's sides. You may think of a tall privet,
weeping among green foliage of others.
This could be one that holds a nest
of speckled eggs whose fate may be ours.
But this is not our concern.
This is not about fathers. It's not
of rasping steel of roller skates,
the smell of oil on bearings
or the sun glancing from such
rapid turnings many years before.
The translucent skin shed by the bull snake
sheds no light on this.
Sons and daughters don't figure
in this. This is not about a hard birth
or an easy death, not attesting
to the snow quietly melting under its surface.
Not showing the deliberate flowing
of candle wax under the tongue of flame.
This is to show us the still fly resting
on the window, its wings miraculously thin.

The Heathen

Sister Mary Catherine, waddling about, filled us
with sugar cookies and milk, feeding us with homilies
of charity and devotion. There was one screed about a man
who gave away his donkey. Had Sister called it his ass
we'd have giggled till our eyes streamed blind as the child's
in another fable. I wondered if the donkey, having previously
ferried loads of bricks and straw, once freed would busy itself
braying and kicking its heels into the annoyed air.
When the cuckoo clock echoed twice Sister moved us
to our napping mats on the warm veranda and dozed
her brief salvation from being holy teacher and jailer.
But I could not drift into slumber, though a frowning Sand Man
cast from his sack all his sprinkles upon my lids.
I lusted to arise and flee out to the sunny lawn
where the sugar maple's golden leaves were falling.
Had I the wit I would have contrived magic jingles
to effect my escape. I would have broken my wishes into sticks
and thrown them to the romping collie calling me forth
into the wild joy of its barking.

Brothers

We were standing, pissing never
to grow old, never to stay sober
by the car of a living green. It held
together the night sky, black
like the dark road that never moved
under us so smoothly to bring us
to the young brothers we were.
Closing our closures of clothes
and opening those heavy doors
of an almost now forgotten car,
we slid back into our mobile tavern,
this car owned by our father and mother
who gave us our lives and stories
of what our lives could and must never be.
Wasn't it cousins and friends of friends,
perfidious and would-be lovers we spoke of
borne up on the hard air of our tires?
In the many-layered waxed car we'd given
the very grease of our arms we talked
in the beery solemnity.
Brother, we toasted the future
by what we didn't say, by giving
our lips to the long bottle's neck.

Skating

In our basement the furnace burned
the anthracite I shoveled into a hopper,
the sound of its worm gear grinding like a train.
My hair was black as the lumps of coal
and curly as gulping blades of the shaft
that chewed the freezing night into dawn.
I used long iron claws to lift the clinkers
of iridescent gray and violet.
Into a bucket I'd drop them and carry
them to a waiting row beside the driveway.
In the basement I'd watch Father,
the band saw's voice screaming
at the acrid mounds piling on the bench.
The first day I strapped on my skates,
I cinched their jaws into my soles.
There was a silver key my father tied
to a shoelace I wore about my neck.
When I stood up, wheels turned to wings,
and I flew to my knees, my temple
missing the workbench by inches.
Father took my arms to help me up.
The disappointed workbench said nothing.
The floor held its blank stare.
The furnace loomed, provider
of the fires of hell I'd heard the evangelist
scream about as he stoked our fears.
But a piece of coal cracked open and out
spurted a flame blue as my father's eyes.

Bullets

When I lined up my brigades of lead soldiers
along the windowsills, I didn't know
why the crawling snake sheds its skin
or muse that the trees that reveal their rings
have been killed. I only played by my house
at the foot of a hill. But once
a black sedan shot by, its grille spitting
October sun. I left my soldiers to chase behind
silver shields shimmering on its doors, dust
exploding behind its tires. I ran as hard
as my will would take me. But by the time
I reached a clearing on Hunters Hill, where
I'd slid down its slate slopes of gun-metal gray,
like fired cannons the dusty car's cylinders were losing
their heat and silver casings lay at constables' feet.
They cautioned me back when leveling barrels
at the targets fixed to a tree, where bullets struck fast
as my heart was beating. I could see miles
from the boom of their guns under clouds that floated
like muzzle smoke where the air smelled of fire
and badges blazed in the sunset's violet glow,
where I learned a lesson of bullets from the tree
filling with lead. When they finished and their car
rumbled down like the sun at dusk, I jangled home,
my ears still ringing. I stood empty shells I had gathered
into rows like soldiers on the ledge of my window.
And as night began shedding its skin,
in my dream the trunks of trees growing to timber
glowed under the moon brighter than the silver
casings of bullets.

Shadow

When I was a boy I watched the little stars
sparking from my cap pistol as the sun laddered
up our Venetian blinds. The ceiling
looked down, saying nothing.
Walls standing at attention cared no more
than the lying floor what I was doing.
From the attic came no command:
Honor Thy Father and Thy Mother!

I had no intention of pulling a matricidal bow
across strings of my mother's heart.
But with my brain's synapse, I entwined
wires into arms of a wicker chair,
though before you judge me, know
I'd pressed my own wrist to the silent current.
But when Mother sat and touched those volts
her shriek was loud!

At the movies I'd heard the Luftwaffe's diving screams,
at home June bugs' thunderous buzzing around
bowed limbs of the peach tree. I'd paled
at hinges' squeal, as Father opened a closet door,
asking, "What's to become of such a willful child?"
I didn't know the answer. Maybe I'd become
a mad scientist electrifying the dead or a father's shadow
swinging a belt through the air.

The Waking

When I was a child, each day I cracked
from the shell of sleep.

I climbed the galled oaks and winged elms,
spitting three times for luck.

Through a field of first light I watched the moth
and the butterfly wake to their wings.

I saw the crow swallowed by sky. I felt
the copperhead's tail stiffen, round as a rat's.

When I was a child I smelled the hair of willows;
I kissed the window of a lake.

What I tell you are lies; what I tell you is truth.
In the dew of morning, night washes his face.

Before I was a child in the morning, I played
with wind; I floated with the rain and sun.

When I was a child of dreams, I heard the dead
screaming in their kerchiefs of fire.

I saw the clouds darken and thunder.
I raised my hands as a steeple

but woke to find only my fingers,
each held up like a radiant child.

Illusions

In a small township in the middle
of a state shaped like a parallelogram
my father owned the only movie house in town,
the former having been burned to ground
it was rumored for insurance money
by the very family for whom
our little community was named.
Under the light of Father's new marquee
where neon burned red and mauve
brown sparrows twittered, pecking
at hardtacks my brother had poured
at the curb, dumped from a silver hopper,
my sibling the savior who fattened town
folk and farm hands come into shadows
from bright fields and lowing cattle.
Come for fantasies to take them
out of themselves as they passed
under a blazing marquee, an artifice
mimicking the searing sun burning
their lives of milk and barley.
Moths of all sizes with wings brilliant
shades of green, blue and jonquil yellow,
some of gold and white of snow, designs
of eyes and shapes of unfolded fans
glittered in the evening's glare.
Moths swooped and splintered,
darting at the marquee's glow, flailing
at the brilliance that to their eyes
must have been beams of bliss
as they battered from their wings
flecks delicate as illusions.

Smoke

The old man in the rest home can hardly see,
can't know what he's doing. Two cigarettes
in his mouth and he's trying to light one,
because he's almost blind, because he's almost
un-alive and has to show his darkening eyes
to every visitor. And yet he says
he recognizes me and tells me of my childhood
I can't remember, that he can't remember.
I must stay a while and talk with him; I must
listen to the walls mirror his breathing.
And now he's managed to get one lit but doesn't
know it, and sucking he brings the other into fire—
this fantastic man with two cigarettes burning.
And some tomorrow when he's burned away
like a last cigarette smoldering to nothing,
in the quiet gasp of his going breath
he will fade like smoke from this hazy room,
and I'll stand again, too late to say goodbye,
then walk out into the blowing air
under the glowing sun that night
will darken like a dying lung.

The Immortals

The immortals never need lie down
on their backs, crossing their arms to practice
a pose of death, or to sleep away the weariness
of our ordinary lives. They would need
no anesthetic to calm them for coming pain
or to cleanse away the fear of death.
In the old South Barracks when I was fifteen
my roommate used ether swabs
in the canals of his ears, so he could hear
the flow of commands and his favorite
songs booming like drums.
A boy in the next room conceived the idea.
Maybe it was his foolishness born
from a half-developed brain
or heat from blazing sun to put
my roommate under a spell.
Snickering boys held him while someone
put a soaked cloth under his nose, and *bam*
the joke fell heavy as he collapsed
and we couldn't with laughter or slaps
across his face or a towel wet
and icy bring him back.
A little death for a military man
was understandable, but we were
only boys in blue uniforms
waiting for his sleep to evaporate
like an anesthetic, to send him back
from a mirthful trick closing in like night,
his breathing becoming limp and faint.
Hauling him by arms and legs we
hurried under his weight.
Picture him spread-eagled and cold,
a nurse recording his time of death
with her shaking hand,

had he not burst back to life in our arms,
reviving the color in our faces that had turned
pale as the bone under our skin,
as we for a moment had forgotten
to feel immortal.

Crossings

As they lie with their stippled hands
flat and folded and we know them
as aunts or uncles, they seem
almost on the point of waving.
And what if these dead should sit up,
proclaiming with their startling hands
dominion over death? Who
would believe it? And who would take
those cold hands, returning them
to that passive position?
All our hands have pointed their
fingers, have pressed numbers
and hung up before saying
our mortal names. We've grasped
and groped. All thumbs, we've
hitched our rides. And waving
to friends, giving enemies the finger,
before we know it we'll be
laying out ourselves, crossing
our hands, crossing our fingers.

Flight of the Dead

The flight attendants have jumped to their seats
and strapped themselves in like *bandidos*.
I'm not sure if we're landing or ascending.
The intercom lightly shakes in its cradle.
For all I know we've begun a perpetual climb.
Whatever's shaken me from sleep makes me blink
at the white lines of light on the floor
mirroring stars I might see out my window.
But for the drone of engines hugging
the wings, I could be napping,
the TV wincing in the den. By now
we have passed above the graves of my parents,
long ago gone on their last flight into air.
What if I could coax out of the heavens
my mother, fire exploding from all horizons?
As we circle the heavens, could she
explain the aerodynamics of suffering,
how it intersects with the parable
of bliss? Would I learn there are no
secrets of life and death, only the vortex
of the one transcendent world?
But as I fly above the sleeping deer in the field,
the quiet birds in their woven nests, I know
I cannot disturb the dead whose love has gone
to ground. From this strange height I cannot
wake the terrified fox from its dream
nor still the stuttering owl. Except
for my waking to life, what can I
offer the radiance of morning?

Flying

My young freckled brother has in his hands
the wondrous wheel of our deliverance or doom,
high above the streets where I had skated
till my heart pounded its circling blood
through concourses of my thin, Band-Aided body.
Here, pressed and held by a canvas belt buckled
by a shining silver medallion of inert terror,
I am rising past the milk-white clouds that never
again can feed the amazed appetite of fear, not
a single time again can be so heavenly white.
This is not a dream but a remembered floating
in the private air of our father's massive single-
engined high-winged Stinson Reliant *circa* 1939.
Its dark blue fuselage tilts upward, the glinting wings
like those of some shivering angel lost
in its heavenly assumption yet striving to warm itself,
climbing toward the hell of sun blazing mortally down.
This is the reality of human endeavor, one teenage
adventurer forcing his will upon the man-denying air,
declaring his allegiance to new bravery, to one
undying thrust into the very heart of knowledge.
And though my fierce brother is unaware of my total
and abject fear learned at the second we stall and slide
for an eternal moment backward toward the solemn
happy place of our birth, the scene of our impending
fall into the never-to-rise-again grounding of all acclaim,
he looks at my blood-drained face; and though I try
to conceal my desperate and comically tortured
concern, he sees back to the years of infancy a child
lying in his crib awaiting a mother's touch,
up through the decades of aged men tottering
on their spindly legs, once strong and sturdy as the struts
of this most costly and very worthy of planes.

And as the plane's propeller's blue spinner once
more points our way to the safe hangar, before
we plunge back through those now slightly darkened clouds,
long before the bumping wheels touch the dirt
of our primitive field of landing,
I have learned to read the spinning compass
of my brother, who has flown beyond the clouds.

The Biscuit Eaters

She snarled at the stove, cursing
the spitting bacon. And after
a barrage at unfaithful fathers
she bammed the pots and pans.
If a little boy could stand such anger,
so can a grown man. Anyway, the sun
sprang up like a hopeful flower
between the two nights. Even then
you could hear a bleating lamb.
She ground the shining cutter
into the *tabula rasa* of dough,
then dusted her hands
in a furious cloud of flour.
Seeing the sun rippling down
the pantry wall, I saw another day
one small dawn stood on its own
like a winked-out star we see,
though we know like a memory
its fire is all illusion.
Let us rise up each morning
with the hot biscuits of hell,
the white flour risen toward heaven,
forgiving the anger of women,
the perfidy of men.

Map Like a Burst Appendix

After the principal's announcement
our teacher didn't say, *Children, you may cry*.
She didn't whisper, *Elizabeth sleeps,*
a small shell in a deep ocean.
Our dictionary couldn't define
her absence. But our *Weekly Reader*
displayed a map like a burst appendix,
and our arithmetic books lay open, proving
the power of subtraction.
I twisted a crank to sharpen my pencil,
with each turn rasping her name.

Even if Beth could have come running back
wearing her dress of printed roses
and reciting all the capitals of the states,
no one could have heard her,
but there would have been shouts at the playground
and chirps of a sparrow ruffled in a tall pine.
The wind would have whispered
to the dust swirling about our feet. Clouds
would have chattered across the sun.
But Beth could no more come back
than the pine tree could grow wings and fly
or the sparrow take root to sprout blooms.

When death ran away with Beth like a wild pony
the sun didn't burn out. Stars
didn't tumble from the sky.
There was only a quick flight of birds, throwing
their shadows on the ground, and Beth
less than a shadow.

They

The Buddha did not ride
into Nirvana on a skateboard,
but a legless man pushed the boundaries
of my child's compassion
as he vaulted himself into my vision
with his filthy gloved hands, on a platform
built upon sixteen skate wheels
of my nascent guilt, though I had not
crippled this poor creature holding
his tin cup for the remorseful's
silver nickels of Nashville
in the dispassionate coal smog of 1939.
I would write this into a letter,
but when and to whom could I mail it
that has not rolled passed me on the hard,
scarred circles of years? Though his coat
was torn and grimy, a cigarette
dangling from his swollen lips, he
commanded the history of the moment.
No king, but a diplomat of robbery,
he sat upon a throne, receiving
his due taxes, deferring to no man,
though he rode only inches from the ground
on the sidewalk of the city he owned.
I wish I had the style of this arrogant beggar
to flaunt the fault of my crippled words,
to make my beholders my subjects
that could but take note of my powerful will
borne by the pitiful talent we all have
for living a short, painful time.
We must all be little Buddhas,
saffron robes trailing behind our skateboards
like serpents of smoke from cigarettes,
as we scoot our way to oblivion.

The Wish

My birthdays are passing. And what can I expect?
A gift perhaps of letting go of dates.

When I was four and happy the candles burned
their shadows across the snow-white cake.

Gouging my fingers into the icing without regret
I licked the melting day. The time has hardened

to history like stale cake, each year gone
like a blown-out candle, leaving only ghostly smoke.

But I come again to celebrate a birthday and make
a wish, that I chew this crumby life until it's sweet.

II. The Palaces of Art

Thunder

My steely art is not for you, but for the busy stocker,
stacking pop bottles like trophies, for the hungover
mechanic and the leather-handed farmer.
For them and for the stooped plumber
and the postman's angry daughters I drive this car
to win. A slithering snake of sweat crawls down
each aching turn of my body, for gripping the wheel
I sit hunched in this sweltering car, wearing flame-
resistant clothing. Power I ride is engine, wheels
and frame, iron rails called a cage. My strapped arms
may be saved from bloody rags. And if I bleed
across the course, black flags wave to cool my blood.
Only the true fans know why I race like fate
around this beaten track of mud, driving not
for silver dollars rolled like wheels, nor for
the trophy girl's kiss and spewed champagne.
But when the air burns with methanol and speed
and fire barks from every header, the thought
of silence blows away in dust and thunder
and I'm alive forever.

The Wall of Death

Some like the wistful smiles of clowns, others the ring
of elephants' trunks to tails slogging around in circles
or endless chattering monkeys plucking another's fleas
or whatever it is they pick. Abroad, I saw a thousand
hummingbirds in an aviary. A rollercoaster took my stomach
with loop-de-loops. And I've seen lions and tigers jump
through hoops of fire. But when I was young, I ascended
a winding stair and heard the ringmaster on a golden dais
assure us a barreled wall constructed of oaks and assembled
by calloused hands was the most daring act of all. I saw
a rider kick his death-defying machine alive to kill
the beast of gravity and ride a motorcycle into the sky.
The wooden balcony trembled as he climbed a circular wall.
We on the balcony held our breaths or screamed as he ascended
higher and higher in thunder and wheels of spokes, shaming
the law of gravity, until descending he waved to applause.
We clanged down the iron steps, hearing a roar of lions
cadged in our ribs. Stars burst from cannons of heaven,
night raced up on its trick pony, and we held in our hands
tickets to the sideshow of immortality where the magician
with his boxes and mirrors made us believe those slain
with swords and saws could yet survive.

Leeks

Alligator Man and Monkey Girl blissfully wed
into an act. Though his hide was rough, his
eyes were gentle. She was the Bearded Lady
of his dreams. They learned their marital dance
watching dancers swaying in darkened stalls
to the tale of a flute uncoiling like a snake.
Alligator Man, basking on his bench,
suffered skeptics to caress his wrinkles.
While Alligator and Monkey were keys
to the show, no audience could unlock
their secret. Theirs was more than a story of freaks,
as the sad clown would say at Alligator Man's finale.
After his demise, Monkey Girl shaved and forewent
her veil to shop alone for lettuce and leeks.
Our Un-Bearded Lady missed their waltzing.
But they didn't try to make a world that never
was stay pretty. We misread all the old stories,
depend on time to turn a frog into a prince,
but time always lets us down, like a tent
smelling of canvas collapsing.

The Ideal

Who can resist the ideal, clouds floating
in an endless sky, fragrance of orange blossoms
wafting at a perfect wedding?

Even in an *Arm & Hammer* logo
there's illusion of perfection in
Smithy's rolled-up sleeve's ideal biceps.

But to show such rounded muscle the wrist
must be twisted clockwise forty-five degrees.
Then Smithy's hammer wouldn't hit the anvil

but strike his navel, the knot
that when tied welcomes us
into the breathing world.

Even the perfectly practical umbilical cord
cinched into that bloody loop
reminds us how little we know of the ideal,

though a flattened balloon
of cast-off placenta was once
a web of wisdom,

the complete map to an ideal world
where blood circled perfectly
like a snake swallowing its own tail.

Circe's Profession

*Never try to teach a pig to sing. It wastes your time
and annoys the pig. —Anonymous*

My dear friends, never believe it.
For aeons I've taught them
to sing in sweet unison,
though it sounds perhaps
like squeals to untrained ears.
But who wants pigs to sing
like bored *Ionians*?
My lovely students prefer
to practice their porcine pitch
where humans cannot hear.
There they gather with their folds
of fat, boars and sows proudly
standing, piglets silently sitting
on all fours. When Moon's light's
an obbligato in muddy skies,
they arise to their song, devising
words from Night's soft belly.
If you listen with ears keen
as moving grass, you
might sometimes hear it
carried on bristled wind.

In Hoppner's Painting

(John Hoppner 1758-1810)

Their heads are round
as children's often are.
In the background the spire
floats up among ascending trees.
The boy in velvet breeches
is drawing on paper held
in his left hand as his little
sister clutches the top back
of his shoulder and stares out
at us in the foreground.
Their eyes follow ours
out of the painting.
In the picture their small
shoes are prominent, his
black, and her one visible
red below her full white gown
points at an angle toward
the grassy ground. His right
toe is a few inches
from pale blue flowers,
three wild blooms
of indiscriminate petals, slight
and star-shaped. We know
they are brother and sister
by their similar features
and their straw-colored hair.
From the almost leafless trees
and darkening clouds
we see it is mid-fall.
The young boy sits on a slab,
perchance part of an ancient ruin
half the height from his knee to the top

of his shoes. Behind the black-blue
and white of their clothes billows
the dark gray of sky.
Under the fold of his drawing paper
we see his sister's scarlet shoe
like a dancing slipper
as he holds an ocher pencil
with which he has stroked
the spire we see behind him,
as if he looked into a mirror
so as not to see us; and yet
we see him poised
to repeat the familiar play
of wealthy children
while behind, in the manor house
hidden, is the clatter of dishes,
servants preparing another meal.

Genealogy

In family albums
there's always the one
we don't recognize,
one we wonder
if even God remembers,

lips drooped, furrowed forehead
foretelling perhaps
our faulty memory,
that tottering old man
trying to find his keys.

We know the uncle whose mustache
still tickles, an aunt with breath of mint;
they stare back at us
with a boldness
only the dead can assume

while we live in a darkened room
where all are dimly kin—
vague shimmerings
in brain's emulsifying pan,
incipient pictures,

familiar faces we breathe
back to life with names, each
whispering: The past is always
future's undeveloped picture,
Then and *Now,* the twins.

Listening

Whether Katy did or didn't
isn't the important question,
though Katy's mate keeps reciting
the contradictory answers
over and over. And as Katy
sits in the grass-green night
listening to her lover
arguing with himself, pulling
the humid heat around us,
what can we who listen
to his incessant creaking
do to relieve his indecision
but question ourselves,
not even knowing
what we have or haven't done?
All the while Katy's mate
plays his organed wings,
back and forth, ignoring
our listening, until
we compose the beautiful
but terrible art
of listening to ourselves.

The Artist of Dust

To the poet there's no
wordless poetry, no poetry

of motion, no reason
to call cleaning house an art.

And though not a speck of dust
clinging to the piano can play a note,

I *know* its artistry
is an overture of dirt.

Even as I push the cloth along,
dust piles up on dust.

I could throw in my dusty towel,
but I won't give up without a fight,

I who am myself
a champion made of dust.

And in my most challenging bout
of dust versus dust

when I'm no longer strong enough
to write my name in dust

may I say to the dust
of myself, may the best dust win.

Madame Le Coeur

If Death steals in as Scripture says,
why, put up a beacon and delay
your fate. But if the old boy comes
clowning like a nightclub comedian,
who could laugh off his grisly trick
more marvelous than any magician's?
Not Sherwood Anderson, sipping
a deadly sliver of toothpick
from his dry martini. Even
in fiction he didn't ask for this final
drink. Not Friedrich Nietzsche,
choking on a dish of delicious cream. For all
his philosophic erudition, he hadn't guessed
the secret word would be dessert.
Pity Li Po, his laughing eyes glazed over
with drunken splendor, who tripped
astern his little boat, trying to steal
a kiss from Mistress Moon's reflection,
and sank into Widow Lake's embrace.
Consider tragedian Euripides, whose
skull was split thanks to a terrified turtle
plummeting from a clumsy eagle's grip,
or madcap Rasputin fatally turned morose
when he was poisoned, shot, and drowned.
Clever Cleopatra, who spoke nine languages
if you count asp, found nothing amusing
in Death's ridiculous sting.
Even that celebrated French whore
Madame Le Coeur failed to giggle
when she slipped on a peach
and slid in through Heaven's boudoir door.

Entering the Woods after Reading Nabokov

The yellow butterflies that annihilate my lawn and belong
to an army of worms with no nationality or allegiance
except to the ministry of death to grasses fly away
and are gone into the previous and subsequent unknown
only the brain of a butterfly may know.

Once I made an application of ammonium nitrate, beloved
by bomb-bursting crowds, in such excessive pounds
it burned away my whole lawn of Bermuda.
But it sprang up from below the earth like the dead
opening their graves or butterflies awaking
from the dew-splattered grass.

When I enter the woods next to my home,
I do not expect to see the monarch leap
with its orange and black wings from daisy fleabane
like a señorita throwing her embellished
sombrero into the air, but there it rises
with the sun burning leaves of the maple.

Hats

I'd like to see them give awards for the sloppiest
kid's room. Give credit to cooks holding the record
for largest number of spoiled meals.
And don't overlook the herdsman whose cows
eat the most pasture and give the least milk.
Enough for economy. Let's see recognition
for profligacy. A thousand reams of paper
for a pompous screed not worth reading.
Prizes for outstanding procrastination should be immediate.
The member of each sex with the smelliest armpits
must be given a shower of hundred-dollar bills.
The world's worst speller, shouldn't he at least
have a footnote in the *Annals of Failures*?
Give a pardon to each year's bunglingest burglar.
The hunter who's shot his foot five times crossing
the same fence row is deserving of a sportsman's trophy.
Gardeners who poison each country's rarest plant
must get something to prick their spirits,
a bouquet of thorns. Our hats should be off
to persons wearing the tackiest caps.
Salute them with a bonfire of stinking tires.
The writer who's always talking but never produces?
Publish his full name in the cheesiest tabloid.
Don't forget the photographer who never
remembers to uncover the lens. There must be
appropriate exposure for him. The mail carrier,
for misdelivering all important letters,
ought to have an obelisk with a golden eagle
pooping from the pinnacle. Let us praise greed,
cowardice, sloth and the rest of the virtues.
For God's sake, give me a chance to win.

Ars Poetica

I know what poems are supposed to be,
a reflection of a snowbird in ice, not
the bird's feathers and hollow bones
that lift it up into the invisible air.
Not wind, but the likeness of wind.
Not the fusillade of kneeling pistons raising
and lowering themselves in raving prayers,
their exhaust gases pushed like thunder
back into the chambers of silence. The hint
must be subtle as sound of an unseen wheel turning.
There must be a slight lean into the curve of words,
nothing like rubber's concrete squeal; the hard road
must be traveled with the gentleness of a light breeze.
Speech cannot be louder than a clear whisper.
Movement must be a single ear of corn's silken tassel
faintly touching the down of a young girl's arm.
But I must speak bluntly. I must direct this to you
while you're here, must tell you the world is not made
of cotton candy. Even the bird's soft sky is hard
to traverse, requiring strong wings.
Art requires the hammer become the nail.

Boum!

Does it matter that Charles Trenet was astonishing and sang
for audiences of Nazis in Paris? It would have had Hitler
known he was gay as a frog. Off to the camp he would
have gone. No more "Boum!" in that song from his lips,
no more swinging hips and lyrics. Thin as Fred Astaire, he wore
a thousand melodies, kept the French language purring
and beautiful as a naked woman before a mirror combing her hair.
Even in war sometimes joy crows like a chanticleer.
With bombs dropping from the black skies of London
songs could be heard across the channel, a voice lifted
to the jack-booted crowd in the cabaret, where cigarettes'
smoke floated like waltzes across the crowded room.
In the countryside where hedgerows grew tall as buildings
and brave and frightened soldiers died by thousands, all roads
led to Ciro's and shadows thrown from a tall laced tower.
The world accepted Trenet for being entertaining and French,
for having a taste for slender young men. And in 1989
when he left, a heart went "Boum!" in his chest.

Guilt

For James Dickey, 1923-1997

We'll never again meet as men,
our words tumbling down
like waterfalls turning
the wheels of breath.
You passed as through silver waters,
through your own reflection
staring into an emptying glass.
With webs of your huge jock paws
you swam below the waves of time,
passed the luminous fish of fear
into the black waters of nowhere.
For us a belled buoy should sound
to tell how lives are bound
to run down, drop by drop, even
as a fighter's heart keeps pounding,
even as a poet's imperfect mouth
peals the perfect poem. Now
you've washed your burnished words,
bursting through St. Peter's defense
with an affectionate bear hug
or offering to whip his holy apse
if he won't throw open the gates. No fear.
You will walk in upon the bright waters
even of your failures. For you, no fierce night
will ever descend. And you shall abide
forever, holding the drink of guilt in your hand,
charming the host of astonished angels.

J. D. Salinger Revealed at Last

You think now that I am a ghost you can find me on stage
in your local tavern swallowing a sword of fire.
But I am the smoke of your tires spinning out of control.
Already I have climbed the roof of the Waldorf Astoria
and disappeared into the sound of honking geese.
You are chiseling away at the walls of the bunker
where I wrote, looking between words moldering
in steamer trunks, which when they are opened
there may be yellow fish swimming out in green water.
It was you who left in my mailbox cryptic notes,
trying to unravel the lines of my aging face, you
pushing your questions into crevices of my fence.
I was the fox that trotted through my yard, leaving
no tracks in snow white as an envelope of secrets.
When you breathed the scent of pine gum,
I was near you. The heart of a recluse is cold
as the fire of longing and limp as a maple leaf
floating in the curb by your feet. Just
when you believe you have unmasked me,
I am nowhere to be found, silent as the praying Buddha.

Swifts

The heavens close their shop of sun,
and on the west horizon darkness comes
riding the wings of evening.
Over an ocean a thousand miles away
swifts are rowing their wings
below clouds still holding
a glimmer of gold while the moon
is biding its time.
These creatures with feathers
no thicker than the falling
maple leaf carry them
so rapidly their name is Swift,
these birds that can fly
a thousand miles in the time
Earth turns once on its axis.
I wish I could accomplish something
so remarkable in a lifetime of rushing.

Aspiration

This wants to be a sparrow
with four wings or a broken umbrella.
It wants to crawl under the earth
and have two mouths eating dirt.
It also aspires to be a fallen sycamore leaf
floating in a puddle of rain water.
This ricocheted from a beggar's cup
reflecting the sun.
It wants to kiss your lips.

The Artist Prepares for a Trip

I leave to the past, the present or future,
or to whenever will have it, the prophets' ravings,
the runners holding their kneecaps,
the butchers bloodying their blocks.
Goodbye to patched faces,
to blisters of fists.
I wave to sagacious critics,
their tomes cold as tombs.
So long to the tears
of held hands, the nights
of dying perfumes. Out
from the owls of morality
caught in their zippers of pain.
Adieu to engraved invitations,
their vacuous words sucking themselves.
Adios to strangers and kindred
clutching my throat,
to computers of insults,
the flatterers' games. Saved
from the chains of medals,
the hospitality of whips.
Released from the burden of inches,
the ruse of memorable meters,
the envelope of bones.
No more the dirge of navels,
the knuckles of breasts laughing like iron.
Empty the sleeves of envy,
the collar of vice, the pockets of pride.
Goodbye to the straps of armies,
the ballet of bullets and fire.
Farewell electrodes of commerce;
so long ankles of myth, religions
of polished spoons. *Sayonara* my temple

of folded hands, my sockets
of eyes, my tunneled ears,
my wormy tongue turned back
from the slit of desire.
Goodbye my empty mouth, my last word
furled like a conch held to a lover's ear.

III. The Garden of His Shadow

Myron Gatz

is still riding his motorcycle backwards
through the streets of Lackland Field
where he drilled us till we were dizzy.
The wheels are turning counterclockwise
as in a picture reversed in time
so we can see more clearly.
Only in a future will we be digging
from the Major's lawn the dandelions
making up morning. As we bemoan
the fastidiousness of our job, our silver spoons
will shine in the sun for the dawning
to which we shall be summoned.
Still in the distance we can hear the motor
throbbing as we sweat under a weed-blooming sun.
Some days Sergeant Gatz will scream
to the wind we should never offend the honor
of mud and rain, we must obey the order of our bodies
though we awake in a brothel of death bound
tight in the arms of the prettiest whore,
and though life may cost us the stripes
we must win dearly by playing our hand close
to the heart, we must defend our country
like a god riding a lion, holding his mane
while he shouts orders to his spotted leopards
following clouds shaped like fire-spewing dragons.
But where is this going? Myron was mortal
cursing us into courage with a Texas twang.
We were pale boys burning under command
of a cancerous sun. It was only last night
I looked into the fading list of my heroes
to find Myron, holding the handlebars of his fate,
had put on his last day like a gas mask and gone.

Alliance

Through the secret senses
of all my seasons
you may see me
like a ghost
crisscrossing
this silent grange.
Across the dusty fields
I drift like water.
I cut a branch
that waves in wind
to point before me.
I must tear the twigs
to make this wood
a flexing yoke
whose two back arms
I squeeze to see
them quiver,
to feel my palms burning,
grasped on bark
so twisting tight
it loosens.
I search the ground
beyond belief
to find what's hidden.
And though I bow
to this forked wand
flowing from the watery
graves of my hands
as it dips, one by one
I leave all fields—
for my work with water
is to walk
the world like wind,

like trees listening,
until below the ground
I hear the water singing,
and then I hurry on.

Spires

Unknown to the white sheep meandering
the meadowy sky, unknown to the
small birds picking in the garden
of his shadow, the red bull will thrust
his nostrils into the spring air
and sniff the chosen Charolais
still grazing, waiting for the magic
of his mounting, switching her tail
at the moving blotches of flies.
Without seeming to notice, her bulging
eyes are watching. Everywhere
the bulls of the earth are ready, their huge
scrotums swinging like pendulums,
their bellowing filling the hills with echoes.
Once this red bull frolicked in a blaze
of setting sun. Today he will come heavy
as death upon the world to make another.
Now he will plunge in the sheath
that will lather with the foam of his sex.
And repeating the thrust, he comes
to the center where the sea of himself
will swim. Now the bone of his flame
will fall like ashes, his body disappear
as smoke on the horizon folding into night.
The moon will rise. And the womb of the heifer
will fill with a future of fire, for the mighty
bull has lain down in the grace of grasses
in the pasture where the shining beetle
rolls its dung into spires.

Cadillac Ranch

We arise from the haze of dreams into first light
to toast with complimentary coffees, to pay
the due bill of night and in a refueled Avis unfold
a labyrinth to find the mist of Cadillac Ranch
in morning's lifting fog. For oddity we must forsake
the solace of our Ford, to praise the resurrected dead,
to commemorate our Savior of Salvage, to witness
these Cadillacs finned against a pale sky.
In a row they stand upended, hoods half buried.
Through these doorless bodies, now given
solely to riders of air, a breeze quivers
like dying reeds of passing horns. Their braked
lights were once flowers of fire, Amarillo's holy bushes
burning, valentines for Valvoline. Now wind delivers
her sermon of moans to frost-wilted cockles,
for the wrath of rain will weather these relics to rust.
And in the black sedan of night, wind will mourn
graffiti that can never bloom back
into a garden of lust. But spring in his fitted
uniform of time will chauffeur us beyond
this earth to shoots thrust up like pistons
firing into wheat, praising the foundry of fields,
blessing the given blood of machines.

Thus Spoke the River

I am the water this man shattered like glass
flaying with a barbed fish its blunt face
the gray of mud. I can tell you how
the sun flickered through a birch canopy,
roots hugging the bank and waves leaping
as he plunged, both fists feeling for a creature
swimming waist deep in my flowing torrent.
I can say he shook the forest with his rifle
to pierce the head of a squirrel that could not
protest its death, prepared for a skillet with reverence.
Rivers have their own notion of what makes a hero.
The pious may say it is to tell the truth and never
curse or complain. This man eating his breakfast
taken from fields would fit that claim,
though modesty would forbid his remarking
upon his own merits of which there are fathoms.
It is uncertain if the huntsman loves his kill,
but the virtuous hunter is like a wild animal, without hate.
He may leave his doors unlocked and his battered truck
at the disposal of a neighbor or even strangers.
He will champion men and women over machines
and animals domestic or feral. He may be faithful
to a religion shooting roots deep into earth. He
binds wounds with scriptures from a black tome
fierce as teeth. If such a man is beset by a cancer,
he will accept it as he does a taste of pork or fowl.
I tell you this as a river feeling his body boldly
in a sloshing against banks: We are one in nature
where a man stands shouting and another sits
silently in early hours of morning, before the sun
has mastered the world, when one can learn
from condensation on a stone.

Barcelona

We're the ones escorted out. They're the two officially patting
their pistols. Outside this railway station three elastic hours are
stretching to five. By the time we're let back in urban roosters will
have crowed or died. Through the plate glass windows we watch
the warm workers dragging their mops and brooms while our
nostrils flare with imagined fumes of ammonia, though in the long
chill of this night, where imagination will not warm us, we need
the icy patience of stars. But only our breaths rise in gray clouds
toward heaven, and our feet grow sore with the cold. Who
can blame a swarthy Castilian practicing his lady-killing English
on a pretty blonde from Sydney who says warm weather's revered?
She praises her sunny sojourn in Italy. The Castilian responds
with a wink to her, she with a Giocondan smile. Once a London
barmaid, she's on her way to a real life in Madrid. Soon they
hunch into separate silences. Now their eyes fall closed.
My sleepless hours are numbing. A rumpled old couple walk
in a small circle, trying to keep warm. Three young men
delicately hold cigarettes and waft smoke into the wind.
A skinhead has kicked his girlfriend in the coccyx hard,
before they revile one another, then scream for a cab, but
return. I count myself closer to the gray-haired bum, fooling no
one with his frayed cloth bag as he snores by the curb. Traveler
though I am, I've not passed beyond my constant wonder. Far
from these night-stalled trains are luminous words in the sky
which must be written for weary wanderers, proclaiming through
meters of danger: The spirit, or is it Spanish for stomach, will be
saved, or fed, or maybe it's bathed. But if I leave these stark lights
where unknown pilgrims grow used to my shivering presence and
do not know or care that I go nowhere for a purpose other than
seeking myself, I shall be surrounded by strangers speaking
tongues understood only by the foredoomed dead. If I walk
down deserted streets, I shall meet only myself, I who cannot
survive the wound of my life without speaking to my fellow
travelers, and to one lone bum; for in this obscure chilled night,
where each is hushed in his own humanity, we hear the same
rumbling train, and in a moment we shall be gone.

Between

He had not wanted
to ride in the air
for years now.
Though fields were there,
bordering the gray runways,
clouds were always
either above or below,
reminders that nothing
is ever finished.
It was only the lifting
off he wanted—the time
between going and staying.
When the wheels thudded
up into the belly
already it was too late.
It was the same
as the instant
when the craft jolted down
and he knew the trip
was over and ground
like open sky
once again had won.
If like a voice
in the wind
memory could be constant,
he would want
to be lifting from ground
forever, being neither one
place nor another,
but always between
going and coming.

Memphis

There's always the waiting,
whether for doom or a plane.

On the New Madrid Fault
we watch and wait.

We know all continents
were one before tectonic shifts.

Look at the maps; the puzzle fits.
Shamans danced and chanted

to pacify their gods and demons.
Our sorcerers study force and stress

and see seismographic scrawls
as signatures

of Earth's buried devils.
The first sign of a quake

will be howling dogs
that turn in circles. Next

every bird will leap from its limb.
Surrealistic trembling will begin.

History will list the startled dead.
But struggling through the haze,

wearing their little badges of
survival, the living will come to huddle.

How strange that suffering brings us all
to a common temple while happiness

draws us into the wrecked and lonely
houses of ourselves.

In This Maybe Best of All Possible Worlds

The bomb has bloomed its gray cloud to change
an unchangeable world. And the Cold War
is just around the corner, wearing its ushanka,
but we are alive and hale as wild roses
blooming along the road, displaying
their pink cheeks to us, the semi-innocent
riding down a tarred line of time. We sit,
three shadowed on a makeshift seat rigged
into the hollowed back of this worn Ford.

If I say we're six, almost holy, crammed
into this blunt coupe, would you believe? Or
can you accept, if I swear to the fading blue heavens,
we're one more than even Creation's days?
On the sprung and knobby front seat, Nathan sits
hovering happily in our cramped summer's singing.
We're all suspended by the moon's yellow light
seeping in laughing, half-lowered windows
reflecting our greed for being.

It's an early Friday evening wrecking itself
into the calendar's oblivion; so we must drink
to honor time, speaking in racing tongues,
trying hard to hold together, to keep moving
toward the gift we don't know we have.
Traveling at the speed of hope, we pass ourselves.
And hanging on the faint horizon, before us in a beam
of our low lights, we seem to see what cannot be,
what should be missed by swerving.

Then a bursting dust rolls upon us
like the shovel-battered grave's and we,
blinking at the star-filling heavens,
are cast out into a churned meadow,

our battered bodies bleeding our bliss. And Nathan,
before he can know the odds of loss,
is wholly missing from the floor of pain,
the roof of suffering. Perhaps his being
an uneven number has undone him or he's lost
because the road rolled like a die over the hill.

But forget chance or the laws of nature
that let a rose hold its tongue all winter, hardening
its thorns, sweetening its breath. After all these years,
though I cannot blow the dust from the mouths of the dead
to understand their lyrics, in this maybe best of all
possible worlds I can hear stones singing to the wind.
I can restore Nathan's breathing, let him ride
again, keep him sixteen and singing.

The Flush of Hearts

To the cavalcade of bikers, to the parade of bachelors,
to this garage door I open and enter, to
wrenches and screwdrivers scattered
in oil on the floor, iridescent lakes without shores,
to the ghost arms of his jacket with zippers ripping
through the canyons of compressors and jacks,
the exhaust pipes and crankcases calling his name,
his voice burned into the walls, the gloves
without fingers grasping toward the ceiling
and the flag of his blue bandana folded flat,
the clock hands stopped in their tracks,
the handlebars bowing for his face lost
in the mirror, and fenders
that give up no answers, for the sweaty
smell of his helmet that can't
lift up his head and the shine of his leather boots
that won't walk him back from a half shell of night
cradling his head, and the drum beat slow
as a stripper's string descending, and for the meshed gears
of remembrance that start the engine to show him
riding among a covey of Harleys, and for the flush
of hearts he'd held in his hand.

Spirea

Neither the imagined roaring lion, growling bear,
snorting bull, nor the archer stringing his bow
high in the heavens care that I stand in the middle
of this garden at midnight gazing up.
In my mother's garden I was a child plucking
the head of the snapdragon, pinching it
to open a pink mouth just after the rains had fallen.
This garden is not so ablaze and is never visited
by the hummingbird with its long beak taking its
life from a silent trumpet. The cat that dozed soft
as a cloud as I trimmed the hedge last spring
sleeps forever under the arms of this floating spirea,
and the moon swaggers around a cloud flirting with an oak
then spreads out his rays like a randy peacock. Until then
I couldn't tell purple phlox from white fleabane,
one named flower the other weed. But parables of seeds
mean nothing here, though being born in dirt must make
for a hard start. I know this: If you mow wild onions
they repay you with stink, but even mold can blossom.
I hear a voice in wind, or it comes from sown tongues
of plants that want to grow like the morning glory.
Though it knows it's doomed, it climbs, not to display
its fragility to passing lovers but to show gardeners
the contemptuous beauty of the uncultivated.

Halley's Comet

Everybody thinks I'm a wise old man because
I saw the wonder but wouldn't tell.
I was clever enough to wait all this time,
knowing no one would believe, since none
were born to hear.

The comet came through the window of clouds
we saw so many years ago.
And, yes, it had a tail as you've been told.
And it was wide—miles across even to earthly eyes—
but it was not white; it was gold.
And its boom became a heavy silence.
The earth shook, then quivered; every clock struck fast
as if to tell time was speeding up to end.

Forgive me. This has been an old man's foolish tale.
The comet's time was much like any other. The moon
raised up a sea of salt. Marigolds bloomed;
the heather grew. It was a time when a drunken musician
looked out his window and said he saw God.

Of the Dead

Of the dead we say he has gone to the far country
or he bought the farm. He's gone to meet his maker
or to his just reward. And though it's true he's gone,
we can't think it so far or to buy anything or he's met
any except his own kind, who are no longer more
than another's memory. A dire stroke of luck
can end a life quicker than you'd think it should take
to sail to death's foreign port that must be
made up, after all, of the sediment of our left lives
where the bar is rowdy and sailors who have jumped ship
will stay till it closes, which is always tomorrow.

How the Dead Fish

They drop their lines through opaque clouds.
Gravity is an invisible sinker left by memory.
The dead look down at haddock that have
eyes the color of rainbows and swim in circles.
Mackerel and tuna dive deep into the sky.

Birds flying in the stratosphere see that the dead
above clouds have no wings. They sit
in silver skiffs assembled by welders of stars.
As floats are tugged down, the dead
stand up straight to pull in their catch,
which they lay out in three rows.
When they finish, they store their tackle
in cabinets with pearl doors.
They row slowly towards shore, knowing
they have all the time in the world.

Salvation

Even a blind man wearing his watch cap like a caul
and walking behind a harnessed dog assumed
a hidden disk hovering behind clouds
must be the spaceship sun due for a slow descent.
Even his dog's sensitive nose failed to detect
something spectacular was at hand as they waited
for the traffic light to change from red to green.

Nothing foretold flashing trails or black
plumes would color the sky and headlines
as clocks' hands clicked and numerals
jumped, when the heavens' blasts struck
ears of nurses in starched uniforms and firefighters
leaving polished engines to be homeward bound.
Only pilots had seen the white wings hurrying
into port and starboard engines, entering
like broken angels above the Hudson's
frantic bows soon to honk louder
than swelling voices of geese.

Passengers shivered on downed wings
skiffed into the Hudson's icy waters.
And from evening's darkness descending
with his shoulders ablaze with gold,
their savior, the magician of air,
appeared to those walking on wings of water.

In the miracle of morning a blind man awoke
to waves of a dog's rib cage, rising and falling,
and for a time the world seemed saved.

Truth

Some things are so ridiculous
they must be true, truth
being stranger than fiction.
The tunnels of blood webbed
in our bodies, stretched out,
could bleed around the world,
whereas the soul, which some
hold to be more important,
wafts from the body at death,
weighing one ten thousandth
of an ounce. Anyone may savor
freely such precision of learning
reading in a grocery queue.
A six-year-old girl bears a baby boy,
or did he live in a pumpkin?
A farmer in Illinois tells stories
from the grave. Some facts are so true
they must be ridiculous: A hammer-
head shark's less aggressive
than a little humming bird. In its way
everything makes sense:
Molecules spindled around nothing
make all the substance of something;
the great masses of black holes
grow so heavy they don't exist;
a blind chick, cracking its domed shell,
tastes its own doom; and my
blood-sucking heart, pumping
toward one ridiculous truth,
thump, thump, thumps:
live, live, live.

The Name of the Rose

For Heather, who died of AIDS

If it's all hooked up, as you speculated,
not foul luck (which it may well be),
it still bears down like a fast freight
while the car stalls on the tracks,
its radio blaring, playing its lowest base.
There's no need to beg fate; it comes
driving bad bruises or good breaks.
The same poison may cure or kill.
It makes one wonder if cause doesn't
always have cause, an infinite circle
flowing back into itself.
In my pocket I carry a silver comb
of memories to strip tangles from my mind.
In my hands I study the lines like roads I wish
could lead me back to you,
to a garden where someone is holding a rose
tagged *Sweet Forgiving,* named for you.

Orion and the Chicken

After studying the burning stars my pen pal
writes me to explain why we get along
so blazingly, which I take to mean we're warmed
by friendship, but distinct like white-hatted
and black-hatted characters battling with six shooters.
I ask her to chart the natal habits of Tim McVeigh,
to tell me if he's blowing up buildings for Beelzebub
or shouldering the swirled bore of Gabriel's horn.
Lying there strapped to a gurney, but revving
the indomitable engine of "Invictus,"
he infuriated families of his victims
who relished prospects of his sniveling.
They dug to their core, picking
at the charred bones of Ava and Adolph,
trying to understand how a pill and a bullet
could cool the ovens of Auschwitz,
how ashes of evil are absolved into silence,
as later would those ponder
whose spouses and lovers had
curled their hair or tied their cravats
before taking trains to a new Babylon
where a September sky fell down
just as frightened prophet Chicken Little
had predicted. And what about believers
who blow themselves into pieces of Paradise,
and can the rotation of constellations explain
Applewhite's passing through the Gates
of Heaven in a spaceship of suicidal stardust?
Perhaps my friend can predict with the stars
the next record-breaking mass murder or at least
send me an account of Orion's hacking his heavenly sword
into the bleeding breast of tomorrow, explaining
how, not water, but blood may be turned into wine.

Karma

If I come back as a silverfish,
you'd need to look quick
to see my face, which anyway
you couldn't catalog.
I'll be scurrying fast
to evade your plucking me
into a piece of scented tissue.
The whip of my tiny antenna
will publish my exile
from old texts of the wise and frugal.
But you must remember—
though I digest paper
which you think strange
and I may seem to you
less than a blot of ink
and am so small and light
I would not register on your scales,
if you should crush me
as I hurry towards a crack
between the wall and baseboard,
the silver of my name and trail
will weigh on your mind forever.

Home of the Brave

Last year my Texas cousin gave up his phone,
because he said in these times no one calls.
But who was I that phoned once a week
pleading he enter again the bright world?
Why do we so fear talking, brother to brother,
son to father, jailer to the jailed, self to the other self?
My obsession has grown, tracing great grandfathers
and great uncles, Thomases through Thomases,
generation after generation of Williams and Johns.
Some lay dying of gaping chest wounds;
others too weak for the field had fallen with fever,
their lungs like fire as they coughed up their lives.
And these now are but names upon my tongue, ink
splattered into letters or carved into stone.
One is famous because he was just or cruel,
a savior of men, a killer of killers. He wore
a beard pied like a pinto, his hair the color of blood
he'd shed by a winding river, some said for glory
and land, others murmured for a murdered
mother, her pale body lying stilled on the stolen
plains, where every swirl of dust rose
like the name of a vanishing tribe.
Perhaps it is better to live alone and phone no one
until the slaughter has ceased, the generations
of conquerors gone home to a purity of nowhere.
Perhaps at this late stage we can simply give
thanks that the bravest warriors would not fill
the rivers with blood, for they knew the price
of glory is war but the cost of peace is compassion.

Stains

I had not visited this farm for years as I walked
along logging roads where I had watched trucks
loaded with great oak and pine climb
and descend the hills. I could see clear
through opening morning the myopic buzzards
circling above me and coming towards me
billowing brown leaves that blew across
the twisting road. Fescue waved where Charolais
and Jersey grazed under the shade of walnut trees.
On the ground, abandoned by white-faced squirrels
declining to defile margins of their furred mouths,
black shrouds of walnuts lay. I was the boy
who tore open their dark pulp and between
two stones cracked the ridged shells,
picking down to the heart of reticulated meat.
As I walk this path edged by chickweed
and blackberry brambles, the sun suddenly
bursts between the branches of the walnut trees,
and if I open and hold out my hands, I may
see the indelible blessing of stains.

Machines

I grant this machine that holds my devotion
is less powerful or artistic than volcanoes
with operatic voices shouting fire into the air.
The rumble of this Harley down avenues
is heard only by street lights glittering by
as its cylinders flash through time never
to be recovered, unless time too is a cycle.
I've moved so long below amorphous clouds
passing under the sun burning in its pit of sky
and all the whispers and shouts of night,
I ask little of coming miles, counting even
wounds and scars my blessed tattoos.
All my torn regrets have faded.
I'll arrive early or late at the corner of here
or there, where all may come to nothing
more than a spill of blood and a seep of oil
rumbled away by the motor of sun
that warmed me, blown away by wind
that chilled. The machinery of forests
will go on leafing, fields rise up from seeds,
and seasons shift like gears.

Miners

I looked up Coal Town, Pennsylvania, and found
the town was gone, though green hills stayed
where anthracite was picked and shoveled,
where elevators had lowered men wearing lanterns
and holding caged birds. Coal-smudged faces
would rise up from pits only to descend
into blacker chambers, trees of their lungs
dark as the black filling up graves.
Though I don't crawl through tunnels of earth
digging for diamonds or coal and may walk across fields
of wild strawberries and buttercups shining
in sunlight beside lakes where white ducks
float, not thinking of coal dust or lost towns
where children once wove chains of clover,
all this too will be gone when birds have flown
from these fields and layer upon layer of earth
and rubble have stacked upon themselves,
burying towns no one can remember. Will it matter
then that friends once sought one another?

Remembering

We have all seen the V of wild geese flying
from winter, then floating back in spring.
In awe we have watched them flowing along
on their rivers of air. We've marveled at orchestrated
waves of their wings, as their honking falls
upon us, the arguments of angry gods.
I have watched the sky drawing dim around them
as they float into the mystery of darkness.

Today I saw them by a lake, waddling along,
leaving the smell from their worm-like droppings.
I thought of the palliative jewelweed
glistening by a brook where poison ivy grows
and of the turkey buzzard, large and grim,
its featherless head buried in offal of fox or deer.
Isn't it better not to shiver and sneak from the brutal
and bane?

Standing on Edge

Once you get used to the idea
the world is a terrible place,
it's not so bad.
Pennyhenge, dimehenge—
I stand them in a circle
on the breakfast room table.
Copper and silver, little monoliths
of Mammon. Some days the world
looks so beautiful
I almost forget it's only
a series of broken stones
standing on the boiling
lake of Earth's core.
Every day is as precarious
as these pieces of change
I've stood on edge.
And we've no more
knowledge of the future
than falling coins' prescience
of heads or tails. But dime
dumb or penny silly,
I count my life a fortune.

Acknowledgments

Grateful acknowledgment is made to the following magazines in which most of the poems in this collection, some in earlier versions, first appeared:

American Literary Review: "The Biscuit Eaters"
The Cape Rock: "Leeks"
The Classical Outlook: "Circe's Profession"
College English: "Memphis"
Descant: "Cadillac Ranch"
Glass: A Journal of Poetry: "How the Dead Fish"
In Posse Review: "J. D. Salinger Revealed at Last"
The Innisfree Poetry Journal: "In This Maybe Best of All Possible Worlds," "Machines," "Salvation," "Skating," "The Immortals," "Thus Spoke the River"
Kansas Quarterly: "Between"
Kentucky Review: "Miners," "Stains"
The Literary Review: "Flight of the Dead"
The Midwest Quarterly: "Halley's Comet"
The Missing Slate: "Boum"
Mississippi Mud: "The Waking"
Mississippi Review: "This Is Not"
The North American Review: "Brothers," "Standing on Edge," "Madame Le Coeur"
The Pedestal Magazine: "Orion and the Chicken"
The Pittsburgh Quarterly: "Bullets"
Poetrybay: "The Ideal"
Poets On: "The Wish"
Potpourri: "Genealogy"
Rattle: "Myron Gatz," "Spirea"
Red River Review: "Karma"
RFD: "Hats"
River City: "Barcelona," "Of the Dead," "They"
Rosebud: "Aspiration"
The Sewanee Review: "Crossings"
Spillway: "Remembering"
SouthLit: "Home of the Brave"

Southern Poetry Review: "Alliance"

The Southern Review: "Spires," "Listening," "Smoke," "The Wall of Death," "Thunder"

Valparaiso Poetry Review: "The Flush of Hearts," "The Heathen," "Illusions," "Swifts"

Writers' Forum: "Flying," "Guilt," "The Artist of Dust," "The Artist Prepares for a Trip," "The Name of the Rose," "Truth"

My thanks especially to Sharon Bryan, Jordan Smith and Dan Masterson for their helpful comments. I am as well indebted to the late James Dickey and Philip Levine for their inspirational influence and advice.

Cover artwork, "Milky Way Galaxy, Top View" by NASA's Earth Observatory; author photo by William Howard; cover and interior book design by Diane Kistner; Garamond Premier text and titling.

About FutureCycle Press

FutureCycle Press is dedicated to publishing lasting English-language poetry books, chapbooks, and anthologies in both print-on-demand and Kindle ebook formats. Founded in 2007 by long-time independent editor/publishers and partners Diane Kistner and Robert S. King, the press incorporated as a nonprofit in 2012. A number of our editors are distinguished poets and writers in their own right, and we have been actively involved in the small press movement going back to the early seventies.

The FutureCycle Poetry Book Prize and honorarium is awarded annually for the best full-length volume of poetry we publish in a calendar year. Introduced in 2013, our Good Works projects are anthologies devoted to issues of universal significance, with all proceeds donated to a related worthy cause. Our Selected Poems series highlights contemporary poets with a substantial body of work to their credit; with this series we strive to resurrect work that has had limited distribution and is now out of print.

We are dedicated to giving all of the authors we publish the care their work deserves, making our catalog of titles the most diverse and distinguished it can be, and paying forward any earnings to fund more great books.

We've learned a few things about independent publishing over the years. We've also evolved a unique, resilient publishing model that allows us to focus mainly on vetting and preserving for posterity poetry collections of exceptional quality without becoming overwhelmed with bookkeeping and mailing, fundraising activities, or taxing editorial and production "bubbles." To find out more about what we are doing, come see us at www.futurecycle.org.

The FutureCycle Poetry Book Prize

All full-length volumes of poetry published by FutureCycle Press in a given calendar year are considered for the annual FutureCycle Poetry Book Prize. This allows us to consider each submission on its own merits, outside of the context of a contest. Too, the judges see the finished book, which will have benefitted from the beautiful book design and strong editorial gloss we are famous for.

The book ranked the best in judging is announced as the prize-winner in the subsequent year. There is no fixed monetary award; instead, the winning poet receives an honorarium of 20% of the total net royalties from all poetry books and chapbooks the press sold online in the year the winning book was published. The winner is also accorded the honor of being on the panel of judges for the next year's competition; all judges receive copies of all contending books to keep for their personal library.

Made in the
USA
Lexington, KY